# Machines We Have Built

OTHER WORK
     BY GIAN LOMBARDO

      *Who Lets Go First*

*Aid & A_Bet*

    *Of All The Corners To Forget*

*Sky Open Again*

     *Before Arguable Answers*

*Standing Room*

      *Between Islands*

# Machines We Have Built

*Gian
Lombardo*

A ClearSound Book from QUALE PRESS

"Machines we have built" and "Light floats down day river" first appeared in *Sentence*. "Another meteor slams into the moon," "Wouldn't that be better: Me with nothing to say," "The joke has come upon me," "To see Manifest Destiny through," "She may never show" and "And if the ground's not cold" appeared in *Let the Bucket Down*.

Copyright © 2014 by Gian Lombardo

Cover image: *Screwed Up Dance of the Sugar Dumpling Fairies: Pre-Atom Smashed,* by Don Eccleston, watercolor and pencil, 2011

ISBN: 978-1-935835-12-7
LCCN: 2014900641

A ClearSound Book from Quale Press
www.quale.com

## Contents

    *Make yourself smart. Not in an obvious way. // 1*
*2 \\ Don't add up to one hand*
      *Blame it on the satellite // 3*
*4 \\ The answer to the answer man*
      *Is some kind of modern art // 5*
*6 \\ Put your eyelashes on my face*
      *He called at my door, // 7*
*8 \\ Coincidence cannot articulate*
      *I was learning to read // 9*
*10 \\ A day that broke up your mind*
   *Everything's wrong, at the same time it's right, // 11*
*12 \\ Don't forget the ape*
      *Machines we have built // 13*
*14 \\ There's a shape over the ocean*
   *Another meteor slams into the side of the moon // 15*
*16 \\ Nothing in why or when*
      *Because all the while // 17*
*18 \\ Everything you do, you do for*
     *Using epoxy to bridge a canyon // 19*
*20 \\ Hiding something from the rest of us,*
  *Begins to fear that I've lost some sense of balance // 21*
*22 \\ Why not dress like one*
     *Magnet draw day from dark, // 23*
*24 \\ Wouldn't that be better: Me with nothing to say,*
      *One way or another // 25*
*26 \\ Trapped and circled with no second chances,*

*On the vine the smoke is on the wire,* // 27
28 \\ *Such good responses*
*Every day becomes undone* // 29
30 \\ *Learn to drive your own hearse,*
*Way out in the water* // 31
32 \\ *Give it a reason or get undressed, give it away like*
*I'm having an affair with a random computer,* // 33
34 \\ *Everything grows because anything goes,*
*Despite all the imputations* // 35
36 \\ *That houses people's very thoughts and belongings*
*Now if you could remember who you were at the start,* // 37
38 \\ *It's all too beautiful,*
*I have crossed my sheltered anger,* // 39
40 \\ *Pitch you from now to now*
*We learn things we already know* // 41
42 \\ *Smell of a world that is burned,*
*What part of the truth is a dream?* // 43
44 \\ *Light floats down day river*
*Now you motherfuckers in my head*
*are saying I'm worthless* // 45
46 \\ *Every raw material at hand*
*No sweeping exits* // 47
48 \\ *Ride the junk star shielded in white*
*Gone in a state* // 49
50 \\ *A perpendicular line to the grain*
*Distant cousins, there's a limited supply* // 51
52 \\ *For someone to come out of somewhere*
*To see Manifest Destiny through* // 53
54 \\ *The joke has come upon me,*
*Useless, like cops at the scene of a crime* // 55

56 \\ I can't do it anymore and I'm not satisfied
        I might not give the answer you want me to // 57
58 \\ Stay just as far from me as me from you
                Time turns to water // 59
60 \\ Too many blanks in your analogies
                All in all is all we are // 61
62 \\ Fat and round, flash, paradise
            No conversation, no variation, // 63
64 \\ Thrown out of windows, for me, for you,
              Grapples with the earth // 65
66 \\ Little fish, big fish, swimming in the water.
                Metal settles in levels // 67
68 \\ Love you, what's your name
                The poodle bites // 69
70 \\ A man on a porcupine fence
              Sentimental Visigoth // 71
72 \\ So until my head explodes into
              Two lights on behind, // 73
74 \\ Clair de lune, a monstrous spittoon
        Mowing and hoeing and growing from towing // 75
76 \\ She may never show
            And if the ground's not cold, // 77
78 \\ Saw it written and I saw it say
                How it's done // 81

*For Margie & Carlo*

*"One tongue lashes another
Until there are no words"
　　—Don Van Vliet
　　requiescat in pace*

MAKE YOURSELF SMART. NOT IN AN OBVIOUS WAY. On tip-toes, chin resting on the top rail following the path of what drops to the street, rolls along, caroms against a curb, spins and whirls as it nearly comes to rest in the onslaught of traffic.

Don't add up to one hand nor multiply to fingers nor divide into onsets. Nothing to doze upon, no dream to resize. Nothing to restore upon waking even if the eponymous image is recalculated instantaneously and then summarily executed.

BLAME IT ON THE SATELLITE. What was once favored now has become a highly regarded provocative missive. Crumple it, recognizing how much it is unlike a delicate flower. Register what sound it makes when it lands in that waist-high cylinder.

THE ANSWER TO THE ANSWER MAN takes no prisoners. Instead, the recalcitrant endeavor to force them to bend their backs so they can scour the ground for the tiniest artifacts — those scraps of chains and blindfolds coated in excrement and dried blood.

IS SOME KIND OF MODERN ART masquerading as three notes on a chromatic scale. Which notes it does not matter. What matters is sequence and duration. Like when to breathe while orgasming. Or how long to stare into an eight ball.

PUT YOUR EYELASHES ON MY FACE and burrow into sunlight. What's not to get? Always busy, always deferential. It's just too easy to placate the spoilers, to say the wrong thing instead of lapping up the tears of a primitive gesture.

HE CALLED AT MY DOOR, calling without advance notice, without calling for a new deal. Not even a new cut. One of us tired, one not. One grew old sideways and one did not. One made it our customary arrangement, our recurring communion of vascular derangement.

COINCIDENCE CANNOT ARTICULATE and neither can it extrapolate. Whenever there's a rise in temperature is there a concordant drop in — what? It's not something that can be harvested at will, or even during daylight. It's what we contract after the rot.

I WAS LEARNING TO READ I wasn't riding a bike. I was finding another reason to fall, brutally fail at going ahead, rushing on, whether to oblivion or not, enduring whatever assault sidles against whatever's saddled and riddled with envy.

A DAY THAT BROKE UP YOUR MIND while turning the corners of your book of abstract forgiving. It's fortunate that knowledge can be summed so that it can be regretted in one fell swoop, much like giving undue props to a signal to crashland without warning.

EVERYTHING'S WRONG, AT THE SAME TIME IT'S RIGHT, but if it's right, is it time? All those noisy ducks maligned. The perfect syntactical unit advancing along the least purposeful course on which to disperse. All that fluttering and all that dystopia, down the chute of a blossom, and out the portal of an uninterrupted rebuttal.

Don't forget the ape when you fill glass vessels with their requisite fluids. Match color to color and size to size. (Don't tell me you don't know how much that tall — see, I'm measuring with my hands — weighs.) What's given are the logistics and I've left home without them.

MACHINES WE HAVE BUILT have been caught erasing blackboards. Now we cannot remember our assignments. Now we have no clue. Now we just have this lousy excuse. Thanks.

There's a shape over the ocean that detects words uttered reflexively. There's always the instinct to provide cover from any detectable ambush. What's taken for granted dwindles the way any last spasm dissipates: dreaming of serenades that promptly arrive lugging loads of forestalled departures.

ANOTHER METEOR SLAMS INTO THE SIDE OF THE MOON and we've entered regions where nothing is explained, but neither is anything hidden. A sort of comprehension you crave: collision and explosion. All loose ends are neatly wrapped and heads nod, comfortable that the metaphor's been gotten. And not some other way around.

Nothing in why or when windows can only open from the outside, can only be glazed on the inside, can only be plastered with story soldiers who cannot tell us how every shattered pane gets lost in the shuffle of heartfelt comebacks.

BECAUSE ALL THE WHILE everyone sat with their backs to the walls, eyeing the entrance, smoothing napkins on laps, asking again and again for more water, less ice, less opportunity to suffer a chill and let go the sharpest of sounds to drink.

Everything you do, you do for the dog let outside, its marginal howl masquerading as voice of the social critic. There's been substantial evidence uncovered about how the system has crashed. Feed the causes and wherefores before the mutt sniffs and turns away in search of more enticing diplomas.

Using epoxy to bridge a canyon is not unlike settling a dispute with a slide rule. Always moving to the proximate, to what space that can be hacked into slivers, that can proliferate until all types of entrainment become exhausted.

HIDING SOMETHING FROM THE REST OF US, then leaving it on a stoop and ringing the doorbell. Is anyone home? (Is anyone ever home?) Let's avoid talk about gemstones. Let's even ditch those fables with bullrushes. Ain't that some kind of extracorporeal ruse? Who runs from when away might do?

BEGINS TO FEAR THAT I'VE LOST SOME SENSE OF BALANCE and brace too far into the direction of the prevailing winds. Begins to find nothing's been lost. Begins to suspect moments are terminally plagiarized. Begins to vomit spontaneously, far short of the goal.

Why not dress like one unless the portmanteau is contagious, the rapturous decline of one-of-a-kind desuetude, our neighbor gone looney at the airport, anxious not to miss noticing the first person in the flash mob who slips and tumbles while proffering an extravagant reduction of chicken bones and horsefeathers.

MAGNET DRAW DAY FROM DARK, and relegate stragglers to appending quotation marks onto finishing lines, drawing sufficient resources to weather any tempest and dispensing with anyone defined solely as an observer. The palliative seems by far the best racquet that's ever been strung, except for the bull's-eye sail luffing, then lowered, part of the whole romance of giving up and getting gone.

Wouldn't that be better: Me with nothing to say, everything to be gained from what needs to be observed, from the back rooms that fill to overflowing, that take their time before taking that first step, before pooling fortunes becomes an absolute *sine qua non*.

ONE WAY OR ANOTHER reduces to the kiss, whether antiquated or not. To the embrace, whether of easy arms or not. To the forfeited realm, whether built from the slice of razor or not. To the notes of irony, weltering or not as all that fluid ebbs on the floor or else.

Trapped and circled with no second chances, the most stubborn make the greatest effort to restock illicit substances. That's what's demanded of them. Not some sort of intelligent redistribution, but spellbinding relief in the comfort of their very own decrepitude. Down deep.

ON THE VINE SMOKE IS ON THE WIRE, less repetitious admonitions. There's a suspect somewhere. Pick from four similarly attired verbs and strike the coincidence. Meanwhile, providence is never in short supply. And the indifferent never in disarray.

Such good responses when a flock of sparrows rummages for insects and finds the less-than-holy grail. Like attempting to juggle cotton balls instead of ripe figs. Like minding the store with the barn door open.

EVERY DAY BECOMES UNDONE and unburnt and unsatisfied, not to mention immodest, but that begs an exultation as well as an unbecoming undulation.

LEARN TO DRIVE YOUR OWN HEARSE, refuse to yield in a rotary, spiraling on and on until all fall down, roll in the muck, and, while holding your nose, make your best shot at pitching pennies.

WAY OUT IN THE WATER is the secret and the fix. Simple. Simply. There's always a complete inventory. There's always some echo that can be dredged, flipped open and served on a plate empty of anything nonessential. And there's always time to ask for seconds.

Give it a reason or get undressed, give it away like the baker's breath. Now everyone can fuck to be misunderstood. Some will move too little, too much unlike loose change. Some will compare them to the staff of life such as it is, such as it ever was before the ineffectual come unglued before absolution and every star that lacks the will to respire.

I AM HAVING AN AFFAIR WITH A RANDOM COMPUTER, therefore the future gets resolved with incredible precision. The future uses those miniature umbrellas to inspire us to discover a future in the future of rainy days and in enough bread to sop them up.

Everything grows because anything goes, which means, in a nutshell, that there's no need to wait for the season to close, that the need to loiter and make rude comments hampers each molecule from suing the residual's estate for either resignation or rest.

DESPITE ALL THE IMPUTATIONS there's every reason to solve the dilemma, provided it hasn't been obscured by a corona, provided it hasn't been deadened by hearing loss, provided it hasn't been rendered unconscious after misjudging the step, landing in a heap on the landing, thinking thoughts that belong to thinking that this could be the worst thing that could happen, that this was the sole provenance on which to befall.

THAT HOUSES PEOPLE'S VERY THOUGHTS AND BELONGINGS as if the one and the other were none other than the one and only. Each volley denotes a move to gain the upper hand, as if one hand could supplant the other until the cudgel's no longer grasped.

Now if you could remember who you were at the start, you would not need to climb steps on your knees, paying more attention to bugs crawling on the ground than the stoned clouds laughing overhead, giving heed to where water pools, appreciating how wax hardens into arrangements vaguely similar to the tactile formation of sound in a cave, to the benign hankering to mount this ascent in unison with the fragrance of ungovernable exile.

It's all too beautiful, too entirely without the whole cloth of shelter of grace. Or within a moment fit to be rigged for a close-following wind, for the right to declare the outcome a foregone occlusion.

I HAVE CROSSED MY SHELTERED ANGER, turned my coat inside out, collected my weight in tinder, taken part in reconstituted memories of washing stacks of dishes, laying them out in the sun to dry, laying down a ploy to thwart the question why they yearn to be born again on the other side.

Pitch you from now to now until the moment when a mote is ready to be plucked from the sun's eye. You were never late, never cause for reprimand. Until now. And the wish was never the certain cure.

WE LEARN THINGS WE ALREADY KNOW precisely because we were never thoroughly there. We stepped into it *in process* somewhere along the way. Interruptions of one sort or the other. Calculated cut-offs, we shouldn't know what we know, but as cut-ins we're constantly singled out and sent to the back of the line.

Smell of a world that is burned, that has a history of hysteria, that has molded columns of smoke into incidental details in the body of the narrative, the body that could not be resuscitated, that opined for resurrection, that needs to be arranged in demotic positions in every room of the house before it can part curtains of erstwhile enigmas.

WHAT PART OF THE TRUTH IS A DREAM? When did you first elevate your feet? Why does gravity preclude, or daresay obstruct, exceptions? How is it not possible to recognize the bravest of faces? Where are the interpolations that sustain perpetual emotion and where does that leave us when they leave us?

Light floats down day river and meets night's brook on the sly. One will say the other's stolen *L'être et le néant*. A few will have even more than enough time. Some will become somewhat more innately sincere. Too many will never return home.

NOW YOU MOTHERFUCKERS IN MY HEAD ARE SAYING I'M WORTHLESS and am not paper to print on. Take count and take yet an additional count by using little pins that indicate the spots from which we hail. Look what distances we have traveled to come here, applauding when your boils bloom and all the rulers are plowed under.

Every raw material at hand cannot justify lingering to admire high-strung sentences. It's not enough to waver from the straight and narrow but to jump from net to net without a wire.

NO SWEEPING EXITS take your mind off these tiny time bombs tossed from the cheap seats. Lively reminders to pay attention to the intertext, knowing that that's where the reader always gets caught off guard, only to realize that ultimately no such sweet thing exists.

Ride the junk star shielded in white while delivering coded messages that dangle from rear-facing mirrors. Every time there's a head-on collision, wires get crossed, gloves sheath the wrong hands that extend outward, clutching at sad, uncontrollable parables.

GONE IN A STATE where the loop intones the Borg's "resistance is futile." Visitation rights ultimately are restricted to those who listen for imperfections in the sound weft from liminal interstices. Even without being lashed to the mast. Even with that "*et tu*" devolved into a perambulatory "and I."

A PERPENDICULAR LINE TO THE GRAIN casts a shadow on the wall: our blesséd angel of the redactic and of the absurd who has come to deliver the rails and ties that conduct source far away from shadow, which has shriveled from such a narrow conduit to nothing.

Distant cousins, there's a limited supply cooked over an open fire, like when the whole family was invited to dine and they expressed their regrets because they could never forget what havoc double-booking creates.

For someone to come out of somewhere and swallow words whole, spit from harder heads who argue semantics lackadaisically as the tide sneaks back in and what we have left is the scoring of a scribe earnestly dashing off grave rubbings of illuminated pages.

To see Manifest Destiny through one ear and out the other. To no longer listen to bound interrogatives. To no longer let yourself be stopped and be asked directions to Sceab's neighborhood. To no longer frequent shops where discomfort is eminently portable, where disorder loses its inherent volatility and luck is what flows in the moments between commonplace and stubborn epiphanies.

THE JOKE HAS COME UPON ME, were it not so, there'd be loud farts and pleasant murmurings, all flush with regard for a change of venue. All the most chic brands of tintinnabulation. Just the right accessories to wear after the impending storm has filibustered daily life. Just before there'd be found no way for succor to stymie progress.

Useless, like cops at the scene of a crime burrowing into another winter, like one of the ones mom used to make. It's a delicacy none can prefabricate, unless, of course, it's left for later, all wrapped up in what pretty entanglements prevent synchronous discourse.

I can't do it anymore and I'm not satisfied by how a drop serves as a diversion from a source. How the source is identified. How the identity is sourced. How the ends and means are neither half empty nor fully loaded.

I MIGHT NOT GIVE THE ANSWER YOU WANT ME TO as I walk right past you, some sort of Tellarini who quite likely acknowledged you *a moment before*, who spun around, caught in the vortex of fated and incomplete happenstance, throwing it back into your face, perhaps hacking out bits of lung and spleen, furiously reversing the direction of the recognition, famously insulting scorn of habit.

STAY JUST AS FAR FROM ME AS ME FROM YOU
even if there's nothing that can tell us apart,
can tell us a novel creation story, can tell us
off and onto the stage, blithely cueing extras
and orchestra with the sole word left unuttered during a lifetime.

TIME TURNS TO WATER and its white blossoms litter doorways that have suddenly gained entrants as they anticipate the great swelling and release of the earth daring to escape their feet and forsake any hope of pardon.

Too many blanks in your analogies will not fill a leaky bucket in the well. Whatever was held in mind, was held for someone else. And so these days all actions center on watching squirrels dance on poles and ospreys embargo shorthand correspondence with their eyries.

ALL IN ALL IS ALL WE ARE and all are done with gravitating to walls. We have the case, the slip and the docket. If we're apart as well as all together, couldn't we absentmindedly adjust the head space? Do we end up heightening or deadening the contrast?

FAT AND ROUND, FLASH, PARADISE that slithers about, steals doorstops and hairbrushes, sends urgent messages, wireless, wingless, without fancying anything save remote delineation.

NO CONVERSATION, NO VARIATION, no bones to pick, clean or otherwise. It's better to fold silences lengthwise — much better to fit tightly in their coffins.

THROWN OUT OF WINDOWS, FOR ME, FOR YOU, into a redefined rain, a shower of unrefined splinters making the rounds, keys jangling, saying, *"Goodnight, tonight, goodnight, good night, tonight,"* as rivers fill with castoffs shorn of guiding witnesses and long-smoldering rations.

GRAPPLES WITH THE EARTH and loses more than it gains by attribution. There's more to be seen by nose than by mouth. Of course, that goes without saying anything blinded by nothing less than the reddest of spectra.

Little fish, big fish, swimming in the water. One jumps up and the others falter. One jumps down and the others graciously tick off brief announcements that transmit delight in discovering the coordinates of ill-formed silhouettes and the lack of hesitation in delivering them to improper authorities.

METAL SETTLES IN LEVELS until emergency sirens call out the next number to be served. In this situation room, everyone is packed too close for comfort. Which is why so few of us can afford to plug our fingers into our ears and whistle as if we were angry at the tune.

Love you, what's your name that's spoken without speaking paintable syllables, without taking pause in the stellar whirlwind, rippling and snapping like a flag in a full gale, standing clear of any obstacle other than the one that cannot be tagged by anything else than what it should never be dubbed.

THE POODLE BITES then tells lies to everyone who receives silverware, enough sets to populate a riverbank, square the sides and finally refrain from mouthing compliments to indigenous bettors.

A MAN ON A PORCUPINE FENCE beats three crows doing the breaststroke across Long Island Sound. Whatever's for lunch, there's never enough on which to become engrossed. At a loss for a flat affect, the accident's just too massive to walk away from.

SENTIMENTAL VISIGOTH accepts credits and returns. No need to pound the desk, demanding endless refills on refunds, where the resilient adherents swallow everything hook, line and sinker — graciously, preferring to bait bears with receipts and cancelled flights.

So until my head explodes into what may be termed an alternative lifestyle, there's no use combing dictionaries for rare words or ultima Thule. Yet there's no way to avoid looking up what's put down.

TWO LIGHTS ON BEHIND, pulling sound from sight. When the brakes release, that's the summons for retreat, as if every muscle could spasm and a smile vanish into mere contortion.

CLAIR DE LUNE, A MONSTROUS SPITTOON
that I call my deleterious compass but decline
to offer to the gods. Well-wishers, do not fear:
We have rags of almost every dolorous fabric.
We are solvent. We've hit bottom. And invoke
every facet of senescence.

MOWING AND HOEING AND GROWING FROM TOWING until the tongue curls into every song left unstolen and the needle fiddles with every syllable that flees and no one eludes solace's misery.

SHE MAY NEVER SHOW her face to the rows of empty chairs turned backs toward the scaffold. What's true are the partly fractured sorrows that may never be tallied, or the wheels that may never turn and the gouge that shears want from unwant.

AND IF THE GROUND'S NOT COLD, then whatever's nothing less than a not-so-firm grasp of what it takes to go from Point A to Point B — as if anyone could be certain of where every single coordinate lies and what colors every moment no one passes by.

SAW IT WRITTEN AND I SAW IT SAY the same things it mouthed when it was too distraught to lift its head, or turn its ear toward the disturbance, or shut its eyes and imagine the sicknesses flourishing among undeliverable deliveries, those exhortations to deliverance that once had names but are now merely horizons.

How it's done when a phrase from a song sticks in your head, outliving the sounds around it, kneeling against doors, honoring selected ancestors, flipping turtles on their backs, mixing all the dyes together, scraping all the letters into little piles, encountering forged consciences, making exceptions that refuse to withdraw until someone extracts from sealed boxes something warm and solid that vacant eyes can scarf down.

**quale** [kwa-lay]: *Eng.* n 1. A property (such as hardness) considered apart from things that have that property. 2. A property that is experienced as distinct from any source it may have in a physical object. *Ital.* pron.a. 1. Which, what. 2. Who. 3. Some. 4. As, just as.

www.ingramcontent.com/pod-product-compliance
Lightning Source LLC
Chambersburg PA
CBHW031205090426
42736CB00009B/788